2000/750

25.99

MidAmerica

D1716452

9-25-17

OAKLAND RAIDERS

by Tom Needham

Published by ABDO Publishing Company, 8000 West 78th Street, Edina, Minnesota 55439. Copyright © 2011 by Abdo Consulting Group, Inc. International copyrights reserved in all countries. No part of this book may be reproduced in any form without written permission from the publisher. SportsZone™ is a trademark and logo of ABDO Publishing Company.

Printed in the United States of America,
North Mankato, Minnesota
062010
092010

Editor: Chrös McDougall
Copy Editor: Nicholas Cafarelli
Interior Design and Production: Christa Schneider
Cover Design: Craig Hinton

Photo Credits: Marcio Jose Sanchez/AP Images, cover, 44; AP Images, title page, 6, 15, 19, 28, 31, 34, 42 (bottom), 43 (top and middle); NFL Photos/AP Images, 4, 9, 11, 20, 23, 27, 33, 42 (middle); Ed Kolenovsky/AP Images, 12, 42 (top); Robert Klein/AP Images, 17; Harry Cabluck/AP Images, 25; Doug Sheridan/AP Images, 37; Paul Sakuma/AP Images, 39, 43 (bottom); Dick Druckman/AP Images, 41; Photo File /AP Images, 47

Library of Congress Cataloging-in-Publication Data
Needham, Tom.
  Oakland Raiders / Tom Needham.
     p. cm. — (Inside the NFL)
  Includes index.
  ISBN 978-1-61714-023-5
  1. Oakland Raiders (Football team)—History—Juvenile literature. I. Title.
  GV958.O24N44 2011
  796.332'640979466—dc22
                    2010017456

TABLE OF CONTENTS

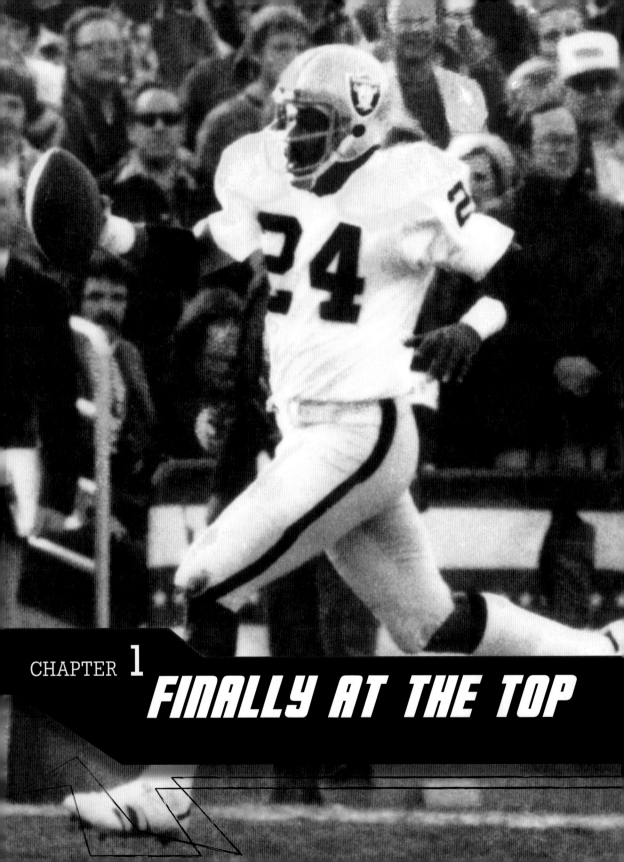

CHAPTER 1

FINALLY AT THE TOP

Trailing 26–7 in the fourth quarter of Super Bowl XI, Minnesota Vikings quarterback Fran Tarkenton scanned the field for an open receiver. Tarkenton dropped back and fired a pass to the left sideline. It was intended for receiver Sammy White.

Oakland Raiders defensive captain Willie Brown made sure that did not happen. The 14-year veteran cut in front of the pass and picked it off. Nothing but 75 yards of the Rose Bowl Stadium's green California grass separated him from sealing Oakland's first-ever National Football League (NFL) championship.

The Raiders' bench exploded to life as Brown raced down the sideline. Camera flashes flickered around stadium. Raiders announcer Bill King emphatically exclaimed, "He's going all the way . . . old man Willie!"

> **THEY SAID IT**
>
> *"Unless our team bus turns over going up the canyon to the Rose Bowl Sunday, this one won't even be close."*
>
> *— Raiders executive assistant Al LoCasale to coach John Madden after the final defensive practice before Super Bowl XI.*

RAIDERS CORNERBACK WILLIE BROWN RETURNS AN INTERCEPTION 75 YARDS FOR A TOUCHDOWN AGAINST THE MINNESOTA VIKINGS IN SUPER BOWL XI.

OAKLAND RAIDERS

With each stride, Brown brought the Raiders closer to fulfilling a dream. In five of the previous seven seasons, the Raiders advanced to the American Football Conference (AFC) Championship Game. But they lost each time to the eventual Super Bowl champion. Brown extended the ball skyward as he crossed the goal line. Within seconds he was mobbed by overjoyed teammates.

The team that could never win the big one just put this game out of reach.

After years of heartache, the 1976 Raiders were the kings of the NFL. A late Vikings score made the final 32–14. But Super Bowl XI was colored silver and black from the onset. Receiver Fred Biletnikoff caught four

SUPER BALL

The Super Bowl is the most-watched sporting event in the United States. The game is actually named after a toy. Lamar Hunt was a founding owner in the American Football league (AFL). He was the first person to refer to the AFL-NFL World Championship Game as the Super Bowl. That is because his children played with a toy called a Super Ball. When describing the title game, he coined the term Super Bowl. The name eventually stuck. And so did Hunt. He founded the AFL's Dallas Texans. The team later moved to Kansas City in 1963 and became the Chiefs. Hunt remained with the Chiefs, one of the Raiders' most-heated rivals, until his death in 2006.

timely passes for 79 yards. He was named the game's Most Valuable Player (MVP). Running back Clarence Davis danced and dashed for 137 of the team's 266 rushing yards. Quarterback Ken Stabler completed 12 of 19 passes for 180 yards and a touchdown. Meanwhile, the Raiders' defense stood strong throughout.

RAIDERS QUARTERBACK KEN STABLER HANDS THE BALL OFF TO RUNNING BACK CLARENCE DAVIS IN SUPER BOWL XI.

A PERFECT FIT

John Madden was known for his wild sideline antics. He was perhaps the perfect fit as coach of the Oakland Raiders. On a team filled with colorful characters, Madden served the role of ring leader with great effectiveness.

The Raiders hired Madden in 1969. At age 32, Madden was one of the youngest head coaches ever. In 10 seasons with the team, Madden guided the Raiders to 103 regular-season wins, 32 losses, and 7 ties. Oakland made the playoffs eight times under Madden and never finished with a losing record. He also led the Raiders to a 9–7 record in the playoffs. Madden led the team to seven Western Division titles, including five straight from 1972 to 1976. He also led them to victory in Super Bowl XI. Madden was named to the Pro Football Hall of Fame in 2006.

The Raiders' coach, John Madden, had been often criticized for not being able to win on the big stage. But on this day, his Raiders carried him off the field. Years later Madden appeared in a special for NFL Films. Madden looked at his Super Bowl ring before focusing squarely on the camera. "In 1976 we won this ring, and it's always ours," he said. "But bigger than the ring is the memories. You look at it and you remember all those

> "In 1976 we won this ring, and it's always ours. But bigger than the ring is the memories. You look at it and you remember all those players, and not only the big stars. You remember them all—how they sacrificed."
> —John Madden

RAIDERS RUNNING BACK PETE BANASZAK PUSHES FOR YARDAGE WITH HELP FROM CLARENCE DAVIS (28) AND GENE UPSHAW (63) IN SUPER BOWL XI.

players, and not only the big stars. You remember them all—how they sacrificed. What they did. You earned it. You earned it by playing hard and you earned it by winning. You earned it by being a champion."

After his coaching career ended in 1978, Madden went on to a very successful career as a TV commentator. He even lent his name and voice to the video game series "Madden NFL." With all his football-related success that came after his coaching career, it is easy for many football fans to forget about Madden as a coach. And it is also easy to forget how special the victory in Super Bowl XI was to Madden and the Raiders' organization.

In Madden's first year as Raiders coach in 1969, Oakland lost in the American Football League (AFL) Championship to the Kansas City Chiefs. That game became the AFC Championship in 1970. Oakland made it to the AFC Championship Game that year but lost to the Baltimore Colts. The Raiders continued to have stellar regular seasons. But they could never get over the hump in the playoffs. After missing the playoffs in 1971, Oakland lost to the Pittsburgh Steelers in the first round of the 1972 playoffs. They then

CAN'T GET IT RIGHT

The Minnesota Vikings were like the Raiders heading into Super Bowl XI. They were a team considered not able to win the big one. The Vikings were 0–3 in Super Bowls heading into the championship game against Oakland. They had lost Super Bowls IV, VIII, and IX. The loss to the Raiders did not help their reputation as they slumped to 0–4 in the big game. As of 2010, Minnesota had not since returned to the Super Bowl.

lost in the AFC Championship Game in three straight years, once to the Miami Dolphins and then twice to the Steelers.

Oakland knew the bitter taste of defeat well. Past failures made the taste of victory for the 1976 team all the sweeter. The Raiders had finally reached their long-elusive goal. They had climbed to the top of the professional football mountain. It was a long journey for a team that almost never existed.

RAIDERS RECEIVER FRED BILETNIKOFF PREPARES TO MAKE A CATCH IN SUPER BOWL XI. HE WAS NAMED THE SUPER BOWL'S MOST VALUABLE PLAYER.

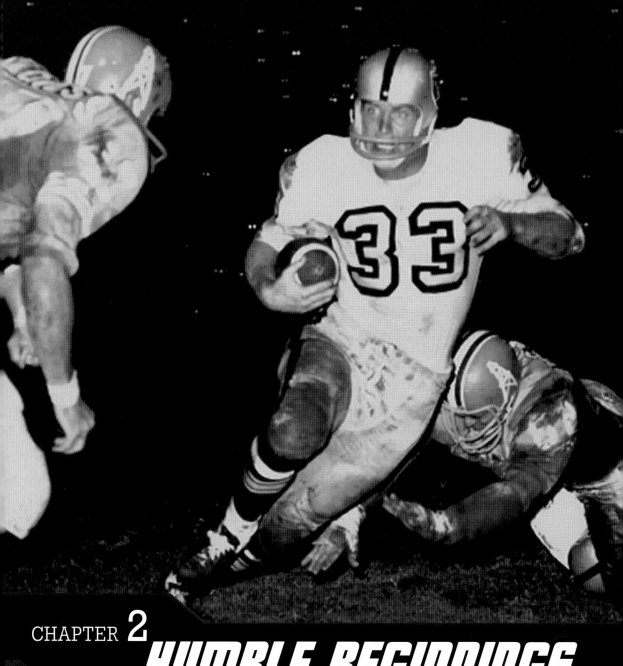

CHAPTER 2 *HUMBLE BEGINNINGS*

On September 9, 1960, the AFL began playing. The newly formed league was a rival to the long-established NFL. The AFL began with eight teams—the Boston Patriots, Buffalo Bills, Dallas Texans, Denver Broncos, Houston Oilers, Los Angeles Chargers, New York Titans, and Oakland Raiders.

The Raiders almost did not make that list. In fact, they almost did not exist at all. The original eighth member of the AFL was a team that would play in Minnesota. However, the owners of this unnamed team decided to accept an offer to join the NFL instead. That team eventually became the Minnesota Vikings.

WHY CHANGE A GOOD THING?

The Raiders' uniforms and team logo have gone virtually unchanged since their early days in the AFL. The original team colors were black, gold, and white. Very early in the team's formation, gold and white were dropped in favor of the familiar silver. The team's pirate logo has undergone only a few minor changes. It has gone hand-in-hand with the Raiders' swashbuckling image for nearly 50 years.

RAIDERS FULLBACK BILLY CANNON RUNS THROUGH A HOLE IN THE HOUSTON OILERS DEFENSE DURING A 1964 GAME.

The AFL owners scrambled to find a replacement. The city of Oakland, California, was not exactly a prime location. The rival NFL's San Francisco 49ers were only a few miles away. Chargers owner Barron Hilton thought otherwise.

His team played in Los Angeles. However, no other AFL team played on the West Coast. So, Hilton pressured the league to add another team in the West. The AFL eventually agreed and awarded the eighth team to the city of Oakland.

The team's owners were a collection of Oakland businessmen. Their first order of business was to name the team. The Raiders were not always known as the Raiders. In fact, their first name was the Oakland Señors. This name was chosen through a name-the-team contest. Other names that made the short list included Gauchos, Seawolves, Missiles, and Redwoods. In the end, the name Señors did not stick, and the name Raiders was chosen for good.

THE "HEIDI" GAME

On November 17, 1968, football on television changed forever. The Raiders were playing in New York when the Jets took a three-point lead with 65 seconds remaining. However, the game had run long. NBC was scheduled to air the children's movie Heidi at 7:00 p.m. After the Jets' field goal, NBC aired a commercial and returned with the opening of the movie. Football fans were denied the opportunity to see Oakland rally for the win. Daryle Lamonica threw a touchdown pass to Charlie Smith. Preston Ridlehuber's fumble return finished off a stunning 43–32 victory. So many enraged fans called NBC that the switchboard could not handle the volume. After that, the NFL added language to its TV contracts to ensure games are shown in their entirety to the hometown fans.

CENTER JIM OTTO, SHOWN IN 1970, PLAYED 15 SEASONS FOR THE RAIDERS AND WAS SELECTED TO THE PRO BOWL 12 TIMES.

JUST WIN, BABY

Al Davis and controversy are words that have gone together well since he entered the NFL. His unusual—some say heavy-handed—way of running the Raiders' organization has earned him many critics. And he has engaged in a series of legal battles throughout his tenure. However, his main passion has always been winning.

Some of the phrases he coined included "Just Win, Baby," "Pride and Poise," and "Commitment to Excellence." In fact, Davis even trademarked those slogans.

Davis also lived those words. He often signed other teams' castoffs. He hired whomever he felt gave his team the best chance to win. Skin color and gender never meant anything to Davis. He hired the league's first female CEO, Amy Trask. He hired the first black coach of the modern era, Art Shell. And he hired the first Latino coach, Tom Flores.

The Raiders' play on the field in those early days was anything but good. Oakland finished its first season with a 6–8 record. Perhaps the best move the team made in its first season was not on the field but in the draft room. It selected center Jim Otto. He went on to play 15 years for the Raiders. He was the team's first truly great star. He was enshrined in the Pro Football Hall of Fame in 1980.

Quarterback Tom Flores starred for the Raiders in 1960. He threw for more than 1,700 yards and 12 touchdowns that first season. Flores later became the coach of the Raiders, guiding the team to two Super Bowl victories.

The following two seasons were mostly forgettable, too. Oakland went 2–12 in 1961 and 1–13 in 1962. The Raiders

AL DAVIS, *CENTER*, TALKS WITH HIS PLAYERS DURING A PRACTICE IN 1963. DAVIS WAS NAMED "COACH OF THE YEAR" THAT SEASON.

amassed 19 straight losses between the two seasons. Things looked bleak in Oakland. That is when the team made a bold move. It hired 33-year-old Chargers assistant coach Al Davis to be its new head coach. The team was forever changed after that.

With a New York accent and his trademark dark glasses, Davis breathed new life into

Oakland. In his first season as coach, the 1963 Raiders went 10–4. The team had many stars that season. They included wide receiver Art Powell, running back Clem Daniels, cornerback Fred Williamson and quarterbacks Flores and Cotton Davidson.

Daniels and Powell were both named first team All-AFL that season. Daniels ran for more than 1,000 yards. Powell caught 73 passes for 1,304 yards and 16 touchdowns. Davis was named the AFL Coach of the Year. The city of Oakland was falling in love with its Raiders.

Oakland slumped to 5–7–2 the next season. However, it returned in 1965 with another winning season under Davis. The Raiders had gone 23–16–3 in three seasons under Davis

and were no longer the doormats of the league.

Davis left the team in 1966 to become the AFL commissioner. Eight weeks later the AFL and NFL agreed to merge. They would officially become one league in 1970. However, after the agreement Davis returned to Oakland as managing general partner. The move triggered a historic run of success rivaled by few teams in any professional sport.

DEFENSIVE BACK FRED WILLIAMSON HAD 25 INTERCEPTIONS IN FOUR SEASONS WITH OAKLAND. HE JOINED KANSAS CITY FOR THE 1965 SEASON.

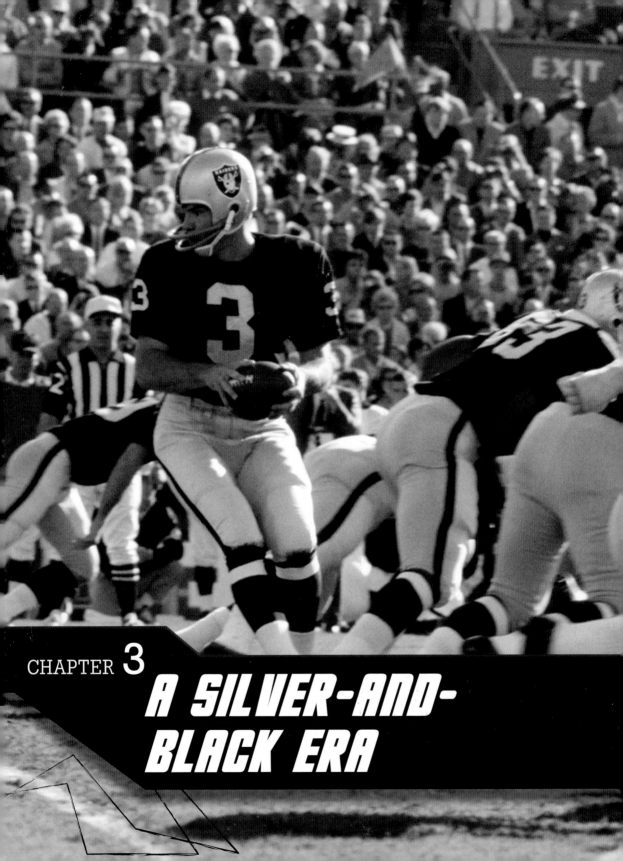

CHAPTER 3

A SILVER-AND-BLACK ERA

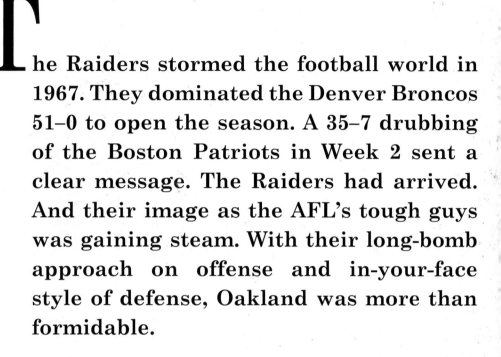

The Raiders stormed the football world in 1967. They dominated the Denver Broncos 51–0 to open the season. A 35–7 drubbing of the Boston Patriots in Week 2 sent a clear message. The Raiders had arrived. And their image as the AFL's tough guys was gaining steam. With their long-bomb approach on offense and in-your-face style of defense, Oakland was more than formidable.

KINGS OF MONDAY NIGHT

The Raiders were nicknamed the "Kings of Monday Night Football" from 1970 through 1985. During that time, the team posted an incredible 24–3–1 record when playing in the national spotlight.

Behind the strong arm of quarterback Daryle Lamonica, Oakland lit up the scoreboard. The Raiders posted a 13–1 season and their first Western Division title. Lamonica threw for more

QUARTERBACK DARYLE LAMONICA PREPARES TO HAND OFF THE BALL IN SUPER BOWL II. THE RAIDERS LOST 33–14 TO THE GREEN BAY PACKERS.

than 3,000 yards and 30 touchdowns. The Raiders scored 40 points or more five times. They also rattled off 10 straight wins heading into the AFL Championship Game against the Houston Oilers. Lamonica threw two touchdowns and kicker George Blanda booted four field goals as the Raiders dominated the Oilers 40–7.

The victory propelled the Raiders into Super Bowl II. Despite leading the AFL and NFL with 468 points scored, Oakland could not stand up to the mighty Green Bay Packers. In legendary Packers coach Vince Lombardi's final game, Green Bay outmuscled Oakland for a 33–14 victory.

The Super Bowl loss was not a setback for the Raiders, however. Instead, they used it as fuel. Oakland won eight division titles in the next nine years. The Raiders played in many memorable games during that string of success.

One of the most memorable games for Raiders fans was also one of the most painful. Oakland played the Pittsburgh Steelers in a 1972 divisional playoff game. The game became famous for a play that came to be known as "The Immaculate Reception."

It was a hard-fought game in Pittsburgh, Pennsylvania.

AGELESS WONDER

Hall-of-Famer George Blanda played professional football longer than any other player—26 seasons. His heroics as a 43-year-old Raider in 1970 are legendary. In a five-game stretch, the quarterback/placekicker helped the Raiders win four games and tie another with late-game field goals or touchdowns.

RAIDERS QUARTERBACK GEORGE BLANDA SETS UP TO PASS AGAINST THE LOS ANGELES RAMS DURING A 1971 PRESEASON GAME.

THE HOLY ROLLER

On September 10, 1978, the Raiders were involved in another of the NFL's zaniest plays. Oakland trailed the San Diego Chargers 20–14 with 10 seconds left. Quarterback Ken Stabler dropped to pass.

He was about to be sacked. In desperation, he fumbled the ball forward. Running back Pete Banaszak approached the ball around the 10-yard line and also flung it forward in a fumble-like motion. Finally, tight end Dave Casper batted the ball around himself, kicking it once, before falling on it in the end zone for the winning touchdown.

The Chargers were outraged. The play eventually led to a rule change. Under the current rule, during the final two minutes of the half or regulation, only the fumbling player can advance a fumble.

The defenses dominated most of it. Then Oakland coach John Madden pulled his quarterback, Lamonica, in favor of Ken Stabler. The young quarterback seized the moment. He scampered 30 yards for a touchdown and a 7–6 lead with only 1:13 remaining. It appeared the Raiders had the game in hand. But then the unthinkable happened.

The Steelers faced a fourth-and-10 at their own 40-yard line with 22 seconds left. Pittsburgh quarterback Terry Bradshaw dropped back to pass. He evaded a heavy rush from Oakland's Horace Jones and Tony Cline. Then he spotted running back Frenchy Fuqua in the middle of the field. Bradshaw fired a pass for Fuqua. Raiders safety Jack Tatum exploded into the Steelers' running back just as the

OAKLAND'S JIMMY WARE TRIES TO STOP PITTSBURGH RUNNING BACK
FRANCO HARRIS AFTER THE "IMMACULATE RECEPTION" IN 1972.

ball arrived. What ensued was simply chaos.

As Tatum slammed into Fuqua, the ball ricocheted back toward the line of scrimmage. Steelers running back Franco Harris closed in on it. He made a shoestring catch and galloped down the left sideline. Bewildered Raiders gave chase in vain. As Harris crossed the goal line for the victory, the shocked crowd at Three Rivers Stadium erupted. So did Madden and the Raiders players.

The rules at the time prohibited two consecutive touches from the offense on passing plays. The question remained whether it was Tatum or Fuqua who touched the ball first. The referees eventually decided the play should stand. The defeated Raiders were in disbelief.

"They said it was my deflection, but I've seen the films and I still can't tell," Tatum said years later. "I wish we could have played the Steelers 16 times a season. Those were always such great games."

NFL.com fans voted it the second most memorable game in NFL history. Two years later, the Raiders found themselves in another game for the ages. This time they came out on top.

They faced the two-time defending NFL champion Miami Dolphins in the divisional round of the playoffs. It was a back-and-forth contest. Oakland took the lead with 4:37 left when Stabler hit wide receiver Cliff Branch on a long bomb to the Miami 27-yard line. Although Branch fell to the ground, no Dolphins player touched him. Branch got up and scampered to the end zone to complete a 72-yard touchdown. That gave the Raiders a 21–19 lead. But the lead did not last. The Dolphins responded with a 23-yard touchdown run by Benny Malone with 2:08 left. There was just enough time for one frantic drive into history.

Stabler hit a series of passes to move the Raiders into scoring

GREATNESS IN ACTION

Eight Raiders who played during the team's 1970s glory years have been elected to the Pro Football Hall of Fame. They are Fred Biletnikoff, George Blanda, Willie Brown, Dave Casper, Ted Hendricks, Jim Otto, Art Shell, and Gene Upshaw.

OAKLAND COACH JOHN MADDEN YELLS AT A REFEREE OVER WHERE TO
SPOT THE BALL IN THE 1974 PLAYOFF GAME AGAINST THE MIAMI DOLPHINS.

position. Fred Biletnikoff made three critical catches on the drive. The Raiders had the ball on the Dolphins' 8-yard line with only seconds remaining. Stabler dropped back to pass. He looked for Biletnikoff, who was covered. So, he scrambled to his left. As he was being tackled from behind, he hurled the ball toward Clarence Davis and three Miami defenders. Somehow, Davis ripped the ball away from the defenders for the winning touchdown. Fittingly, the game was dubbed the "Sea of Hands" game.

CHAPTER 4

AGAINST ALL ODDS

The 1980 Oakland Raiders did not have the look of a Super Bowl champion. In the fifth game of the season, starting quarterback Dan Pastorini suffered a broken leg. The Raiders called on 33-year-old castoff Jim Plunkett. Plunkett promptly threw five interceptions in a 31–17 loss to the Kansas City Chiefs. Oakland slumped to 2–3.

The Raiders always believed in second chances. Plunkett had been a Heisman Trophy winner from Stanford University. But he had struggled throughout his professional career to that point. This was his chance. And, boy, did he take it.

Plunkett led the Raiders on a historic march. The team won nine of its 11 remaining games. The Raiders even secured a wild-card spot in the playoffs. No wild-card team had ever won the Super Bowl before. The Raiders went about changing that. They

RAIDERS QUARTERBACK JIM PLUNKETT THROWS A BALL DOWNFIELD AGAINST THE SAN DIEGO CHARGERS IN 1981.

ANOTHER CHANCE IS ALL HE NEEDED

Expectations were high for quarterback Jim Plunkett when he came out of college. The New England Patriots drafted him number one overall in 1971. But he played five mostly forgettable seasons with the Patriots. He then played two more mediocre years with the San Francisco 49ers.

In 1978, he joined the Oakland Raiders. Plunkett's career was widely considered a bust at that point. He saw very little action during his first two seasons. But then he took over after starter Dan Pastorini was injured. Once he got the job, he did not let go until injuries derailed his career. Plunkett led the Raiders to two Super Bowl victories. He is the only eligible quarterback in league history to win two Super Bowls and not be named to the Pro Football Hall of Fame.

advanced from the first round after drubbing the Houston Oilers 27–7. It appeared Oakland's season was about to end on an ice-covered field in Cleveland the next week. The Raiders led the Browns 14–12. But Cleveland had one last drive. Behind quarterback Brian Sipe, the Browns moved the ball to the Oakland 13 with less than a minute to play.

All Cleveland needed was a field goal. But the frosty conditions made that no guarantee. Also on the Browns' minds was the fact that 6 foot 7 inch Ted Hendricks had blocked an extra point earlier in the game. The Browns decided to throw a pass into the end zone, hoping to catch Oakland by surprise. But safety Mike Davis had other plans. He stepped in front of tight end Ozzie Newsome and made an interception to seal

OAKLAND SAFETY MIKE DAVIS INTERCEPTS A PASS WITH 49 SECONDS
LEFT IN A 1980 PLAYOFF GAME AGAINST THE CLEVELAND BROWNS.

the victory. Davis remembered the silence of the 77,655 fans in attendance.

"It was eerie," Davis said. "There was almost no sound."

The next week, Oakland played its third straight road playoff game. The Raiders traveled to San Diego for the AFC Championship Game. Plunkett threw touchdowns to Raymond Chester and Kenny King. He ran for another—all in the first quarter. The Raiders held off the Chargers, 34–27. The victory set up a Super Bowl showdown against the Philadelphia Eagles. The Eagles had already defeated the Raiders 10–7 earlier in the season.

But Super Bowl XV was not a close contest. Plunkett threw three touchdowns, including two to Cliff Branch. Plunkett was also named Super Bowl MVP. Oakland linebacker Rod Martin was another candidate for the award. He intercepted Eagles quarterback Ron Jaworski three times.

"The Eagles somehow felt they could exploit Rod Martin," Hendricks said. "They decided to attack the right side of our defense, away from me. They tested Rod the whole game, and all they got out of it was three interceptions."

The Raiders had done what no other football team had done before. They won the Super Bowl as a wild-card team, bucking all odds. They were on top of the football world again. But not long after, in 1982, they headed south. Owner Al Davis won a lengthy legal battle with the NFL. He moved the Raiders from Oakland to Los Angeles. But their winning ways went with them.

THE RAIDERS DEFENSE WRAPS UP PHILADELPHIA EAGLES RUNNING BACK WILBERT MONTGOMERY IN SUPER BOWL XV. OAKLAND WON 27–10.

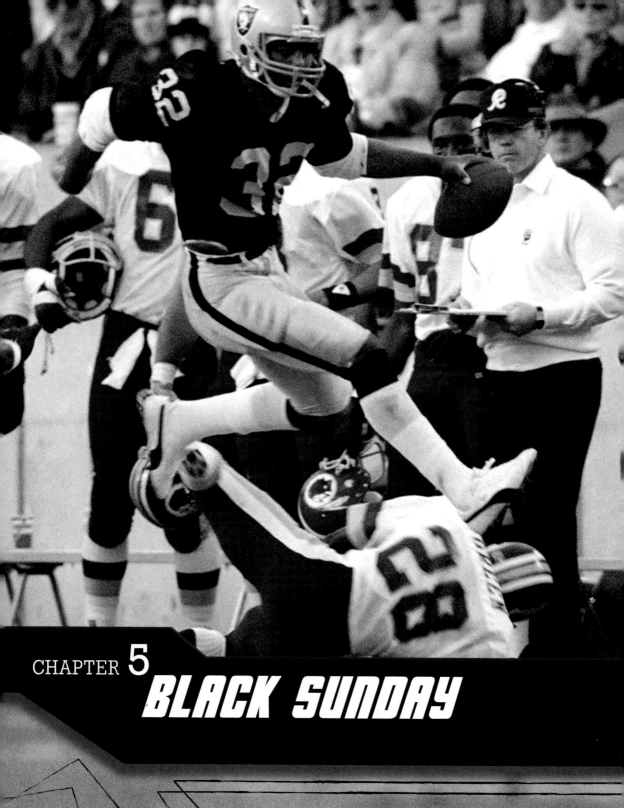

CHAPTER 5

BLACK SUNDAY

The Raiders' second season in Los Angeles was in 1983. All the pieces were in place for another run at the championship. Jim Plunkett was the team's established leader at quarterback. Running back Marcus Allen was quickly becoming one of the best. Tight end Todd Christensen was nearly unstoppable, too. He made first-team All-Pro that season with 92 catches for 1,247 yards and 12 touchdowns.

The Raiders averaged more than 27 points per game. They roared into the playoffs as AFC West champs with a 12–4 record. In the playoffs, Los Angeles kept rolling with easy wins over the Pittsburgh Steelers (38–10) and Seattle Seahawks (30–14).

Next up was Super Bowl XVIII. The opponent was the defending champion Washington Redskins. Washington scored a then-NFL record 541 points that season. Even the most dedicated Raiders fans could not see what was to come.

MARCUS ALLEN HIGH STEPS OVER A REDSKINS DEFENDER IN SUPER BOWL XVII. ALLEN SET A THEN-SUPER BOWL RECORD WITH 191 RUSHING YARDS.

In a game dubbed "Black Sunday," the Raiders dominated from start to finish. Allen ran for a then-Super Bowl record 191 yards and two touchdowns. Allen also made the game's signature play in the third quarter. He took a handoff and navigated to his left only to find the path blocked. He quickly reversed his direction. Allen eluded tacklers until he found a crack. He then shot through the Redskins defense and sprinted 74 yards for a touchdown. That gave the Raiders a gigantic 35–9 lead en route to a 38–9 win.

While Allen's play is the signature moment of Super Bowl XVIII, it was a play before halftime that might have been the most crucial. With only 12 seconds left in the half, Washington quarterback Joe Theismann tried to throw a screen pass. Instead, Oakland linebacker Jack Squirek intercepted the ball and returned it for a touchdown to give the Raiders a 21–3 halftime lead. The play deflated the favored Redskins.

Washington had used the same play in a victory over Los Angeles earlier in the season. This time, the Raiders were prepared. Linebackers coach Charlie Sumner sent Squirek

HENRY LAWRENCE (70) BLOCKS A WASHINGTON REDSKINS DEFENDER FOR RAIDERS RUNNING BACK MARCUS ALLEN DURING SUPER BOWL XVIII.

onto the field as substitution prior to the play. Squirek had specific instructions to cover running back Joe Washington in case of a screen pass. It worked perfectly. Squirek had never scored a touchdown in college or in the pros. He was almost as shocked as the Redskins. "I must've had 2,000 pounds [of teammates] jump on top of me," he said. "I never got a chance to spike [the ball]."

MR. RAIDER

Tim Brown's magnificent career with the Silver and Black earned him the moniker "Mr. Raider." The Heisman Trophy winner out of Notre Dame played 16 seasons with the Raiders. His 240 games with the Raiders are a team best. He also holds nearly every team receiving record. As a Raider, Brown caught 1,070 passes for 14,734 yards and 99 touchdowns. He played one final season with Tampa Bay. His 100 receiving touchdowns tie him with Steve Largent for sixth all-time. He ranks fourth in career receiving yards. Brown played with the Raiders from 1988 to 2003 and was a nine-time Pro Bowler.

The Raiders made the playoffs the following two years, but the magic in Los Angeles soon faded. From 1986–1994, the team won 10 games or more only twice. In 1995, Al Davis again shocked the football world by moving his club back to its original home in Oakland. The glory years in Oakland were far removed, though. The team hired and replaced coaches regularly.

The lone bright spot during the team's return to the Bay Area came during the Jon Gruden/Bill Callahan era. Coach Gruden's short, controlled passing attack meshed well with quarterback Rich Gannon. The team won back-to-back division titles in 2000 and 2001. Heart-breaking losses to the Baltimore Ravens in the 2000 AFC Championship and to the New England Patriots in the 2001 Divisional Playoffs marked the end of Gruden's time as Oakland coach.

Callahan took over as coach in 2002. He led the team all the way to Super Bowl XXXVII. It was the team's fifth Super Bowl appearance. Ironically, Oakland lost to Gruden's Tampa Bay Buccaneers 48–21. The 2002 season was Gruden's first as coach of Tampa Bay. He had

OAKLAND FANS WELCOMED THE RAIDERS BACK IN 1995. RAIDERS FANS ARE KNOWN FOR THEIR HARDCORE SUPPORT OF THEIR TEAM.

THE TUCK RULE

Adding to their long list of memorable games, the Raiders came out on the wrong side of a game now known as the "Tuck Rule Game." In January 2002, Oakland played at New England in the playoffs. The Raiders led 13–10 as the Patriots drove down the field late in the game. Raiders cornerback Charles Woodson blitzed Patriots quarterback Tom Brady, hitting him hard and jarring the ball free. Oakland's Greg Biekert pounced on the ball, seemingly ending the game.

Instead, the referees ruled that Brady had pumped the ball without securing it back into his body. So, the play was an incomplete pass. New England eventually won in overtime. The Patriots went on to win the Super Bowl. The head of the NFL's officiating department agreed that the play was called correctly according to the tuck rule. Oakland players had a different outlook. "We didn't lose this game," said linebacker William Thomas. "It was stolen from us."

been traded by Oakland to the Buccaneers in exchange for four draft picks.

Victories have since been fleeting for the Raiders. Oakland has not won more than five games in any season from 2003 to 2009. Yet this proud franchise is determined to regain its winning ways. And Davis vows that a revival is near.

"We'll be back. The Raiders will be back. I just know that the fire that burns brightest in this building is the will to win. And we will win," proclaimed Davis.

RAIDERS RECEIVER JERRY RICE RUNS IN A TOUCHDOWN PASS IN SUPER BOWL XXXVII. BUT THE RAIDERS LOST TO THE TAMPA BAY BUCCANEERS 48–21.

TIMELINE

1960	The Raiders play their first game, losing to the Houston Oilers 37–22 on September 11.
1963	Al Davis is named coach and general manager on January 15.
1966	The Raiders play their first game in Oakland-Alameda County Coliseum on September 18.
1968	The Green Bay Packers defeat the Raiders 33–14 in Super Bowl II on January 14. Oakland wins the famous "*Heidi* game" by scoring twice in the final minute to defeat the New York Jets 43–32 on November 17.
1969	John Madden is named Raiders coach on February 4.
1972	The Pittsburgh Steelers defeat Oakland 13–7 on a controversial pass deflection, known as "The Immaculate Reception," on December 23.
1977	Fred Biletnikoff catches four passes for 79 yards and is named Super Bowl MVP as the Raiders win their first Super Bowl with a 32–14 victory over the Minnesota Vikings in Super Bowl XI on January 9.
1979	John Madden retires as coach on January 4. The Raiders appoint Tom Flores as coach on February 8.

1981
Jim Plunkett is named Super Bowl MVP as Oakland defeats the Philadelphia Eagles 27–10 for its second Super Bowl title on January 25.

1982
The Raiders move from Oakland to Los Angeles. They defeat the San Diego Chargers 28–24 in their first home game in Los Angeles.

1984
Marcus Allen runs for a Super Bowl-record 191 yards and is named Super Bowl MVP as the Raiders defeat the Washington Redskins 38–9 in Super Bowl XVIII on January 22.

1995
The Raiders sign an agreement on August 7 to return to Oakland.

1998
Jon Gruden, at age 34, is named Raiders coach.

2002
The Raiders lose to the New England Patriots 16–13 in overtime of a divisional playoff in a game known as the "Tuck Rule Game" on January 19.

2002
Bill Callahan takes over as Oakland's coach.

2003
The Raiders fall to the Tampa Buccaneers 48–21 in Super Bowl XXXVII on January 26.

2009
For the seventh straight season, the Raiders fail to win more than five games.

QUICK STATS

FRANCHISE HISTORY
Oakland Señors (AFL) 1960
Oakland Raiders (AFL) 1960–69
Los Angeles Raiders 1982–94
Oakland Raiders 1970–81; 1995–

SUPER BOWLS
(wins in bold)
1967 (II), **1976 (XI)**, **1980 (XV)**,
1983 (XVIII), 2002 (XXXVII)

AFL CHAMPIONSHIP GAMES
(1960–69; wins in bold)
1967, 1968, 1969

AFC CHAMPIONSHIP GAMES
(since 1970 AFL-NFL merger)
1970, 1973, 1974, 1975, 1976, 1977,
1980, 1983, 1990, 2000, 2002

DIVISION CHAMPIONSHIPS
(since 1970 AFL-NFL merger)
1970, 1972, 1973, 1974, 1975, 1976,
1983, 1985, 1990, 2000, 2001, 2002

KEY PLAYERS
(position, seasons with team)
Marcus Allen (RB, 1982–1992)
Fred Biletnikoff (WR, 1965–1978)
George Blanda (QB/K, 1967–1975)
Tim Brown (WR, 1988–2003)
Willie Brown (DB, 1967–1978)
Dave Casper (TE, 1974–1980, 1984)
Ted Hendricks (LB, 1975–1983)
Howie Long (DE, 1981–1993)
Jim Otto (C, 1960–1974)
Jim Plunkett (QB, 1979–86)
Art Shell (T, 1968–1982)
Ken Stabler (QB, 1968–1979)
Jack Tatum (S, 1971–1979)
Gene Upshaw (G, 1967–1981)

KEY COACHES
John Madden (1969–1978):
    103–32–7; 9–7 (playoffs)
Tom Flores (1979–1987): 83–53;
    8–3 (playoffs)

HOME FIELDS
Oakland-Alameda County Coliseum
    (1966–81; 1995–)
Los Angeles Memorial Coliseum
    (1982–94)
Frank Youell Field (1962–65)
Candlestick Park (1960–61)
Kezar Stadium (1960)

* All statistics through 2009 season

QUOTES AND ANECDOTES

Perhaps no other player in the 1960s portrayed the Raiders' image more than defensive end "Big" Ben Davidson. At 6 feet 8 inches and sporting a handlebar mustache, Davidson looked fierce. He also played that way. Davidson terrorized opposing quarterbacks for the Raiders from 1964 to 1971. One particular incident is often replayed when the Raiders play the Chiefs. In 1970, the Chiefs appeared to have victory in hand when quarterback Len Dawson ran for a late-game first down. Davidson lunged on top of Dawson and was flagged for spearing. The Chiefs retaliated for what they deemed a dirty play. The ensuing fight resulted in offsetting penalties and negated the play. The Chiefs eventually had to punt, and Oakland rallied for the tying field goal. Davidson was a three-time AFL All-Star and made first-team All-AFL once.

"If my mother put on a helmet and shoulder pads and a uniform that wasn't the same as the one I was wearing, I'd run over her if she was in my way. And I love my mother." — Bo Jackson

Hall of Fame defensive end Howie Long finished his Raiders career with 84 career sacks. But he also had 7.5 in 1981—one year before sacks became an official NFL statistic.

"Hey, the offensive linemen are the biggest guys on the field. They're bigger than everybody else. And that's what makes them the biggest guys on the field." — John Madden

"To win, I'd run over Joe's mom, too," — linebacker Matt Millen, in response to Redskins lineman Joe Jacoby saying that he'd run over his own mother to win the Super Bowl.

GLOSSARY

All-Pro

An award given to the top players at their position regardless of their conference. It is a high honor as there are fewer spots on the All-Pro team than on the Pro Bowl teams.

draft

A system used by professional sports leagues to select new players in order to spread incoming talent among all teams.

franchise

An entire sports organization, including players, coaches, and staff.

hall of fame

A place built to honor noteworthy achievements by athletes in their respective sports.

Heisman Trophy

An award given to the top college football player each year.

managing general partner

A term indicating that an owner is also involved in the day-to-day operations of the business.

merge

To unite into a single body.

moniker

A nickname.

pass deflection

The act of a defensive player preventing a completed pass by misdirecting the flight of the ball.

screen pass

A play in which the quarterback drops back as if to throw a long pass while the linemen allow defenders to rush him. The quarterback then dumps a short pass off to a receiver or running back, who then has the aid of linemen to advance the football.

spike

The act of throwing the ball to the ground.

TV contract

An agreement in which the NFL is paid by television networks for the exclusive rights to air their games.

FOR MORE INFORMATION

Further Reading

Flores, Tom, with Matt Fulks. *Tom Flores' tales from the Oakland Raiders*. Champaign, IL: Sports Pub., 2007.

MacCambridge, Michael. *America's Game: The Epic Story of How Pro Football Captured a Nation*. New York: Random House, 2004.

Sports Illustrated. *The Football Book Expanded Edition*. New York: Sports Illustrated Books, 2009.

Web Links

To learn more about the Oakland Raiders, visit ABDO Publishing Company online at **www.abdopublishing.com**. Web sites about the Raiders are featured on our Book Links page. These links are routinely monitored and updated to provide the most current information available.

Places to Visit

Bay Area Sports Hall of Fame
201 Spear Street, Suite 1150
San Francisco, CA 94105
415-296-5607
http://www.bashof.org/
This hall of fame enshrines the great athletes of the Bay Area (San Francisco and Oakland) and helps children participate in sports. The organization does not have a museum.

Oakland-Alameda County Coliseum
7000 Coliseum Way
Oakland, CA 94621
510-569-2121
http://www.coliseum.com/events/sports.php
The home to the Oakland Raiders and the Oakland A's of Major League Baseball.

Pro Football Hall of Fame
2121 George Halas Drive Northwest
Canton, OH 44708
330-456-8207
http://www.profootballhof.com/
This hall of fame and museum highlights the greatest players and moments in the history of the National Football League. Twenty people affiliated with the Raiders are enshrined, including Fred Biletnikoff, Al Davis, John Madden, and Art Shell.

INDEX

About the Author

Tom Needham lives with his wife and two daughters in Charlotte, North Carolina. He is a former sports editor at the *Herald-Star* newspaper in Steubenville, Ohio. He won a 1998 West Virginia Associated Press Best Sports News Writing Award. His writing has appeared in American Football Monthly magazine and Street & Smith's Specialty Publications. He has written three sports-themed books for young readers.